Charles R. Swindoll

RECOVERING A PIONEER SPIRIT

NEHEMIAH

A MODEL OF PIONEER

DETERMINATION

Fifth in a series of five mini-books,
based on the lives of biblical characters
who modeled an attitude of fortitude
that needs to be recovered.

INSIGHT FOR LIVING

Printed in the United States of America.

Book designed by Jerry Ford
Cover illustration by Diana Vasquez

*Committed to Excellence in Communicating
Biblical Truth and Its Application*

INTRODUCTION

In this brief yet poignant series of mini-books on "Recovering a Pioneer Spirit," we have looked at the lives of four significant characters in the Scriptures. As we examined the life of Abraham, we found a man whose life was marked by *faith* . . . strong, consistent, exemplary faith. Next came David as he took on Goliath, the notorious giant from Gath. Young David modeled *courage*, the kind seldom found in our era of compromise and softhearted diplomacy. Esther followed, the Jewish queen whose *independence* of spirit saved her people from annihilation at the hands of the Persians. We then blew the dust off the ancient account of Moses, the man of *vision,* whom God used to lead the Exodus out of Egypt.

For our final biographical glimpse at one more biblical "pioneer," we turn our attention to Nehemiah, a magnificent example of *determination.* Just the mention of that word reminds us of a character quality that is rapidly becoming extinct. Ours is a day of thin-skinned soldiers who are quick to quit when the going gets rough. How greatly we need men and women in the ranks of the righteous who are committed to enduring rather than escaping hardship.

Like the adventurous, leather-skinned
pioneers of yesteryear, strong-hearted
people of God give us needed motivation to stay on the trail and face
life's difficulties head-on.

I know of few qualities I admire
more than determination. Not only
is it essential for seeing a project
through to completion, but it stirs
our hope and keeps us positive dur-
ing the long haul. Because it is so
contagious, others are encouraged
not to cave in when the going be-
comes arduous and demanding. And
as we shall discover in our study of
Nehemiah, determination and leadership go hand in hand. Those being
led can easily lose heart unless the

leader represents a never-say-die attitude that keeps the goal in clear focus.

My desire is that you will find fresh hope in the pages that follow. In addition, may the can-do model of Nehemiah convince you that you can make it through the crisis you face today . . . and because you can, *you must.*

Chuck

Chuck Swindoll
Fullerton, California

NEHEMIAH

A MODEL OF PIONEER

DETERMINATION

There is an old gospel song that encourages Christians to keep our eyes on the ultimate destination —heaven. Using terminology familiar to those ancient Hebrews who had escaped Egyptian bondage and were making their way toward the "Promised Land" of Canaan, the songwriter portrays us as standing on the banks of the Jordan River, looking longingly to the other side. Once we cross that final river of death, peace and joy are ours to claim.

On Jordan's stormy banks I stand,
And cast a wishful eye
To Canaan's fair and happy land,
Where my possessions lie.

I am bound for the promised land,
I am bound for the promised land;
O who will come and go with me?
I am bound for the promised land.[1]

Doesn't that sound wonderful? Almost too good to be true? But it *is* the real hope of every believer— that "fair and happy land" will be ours to enjoy forever. In that eternal home there will be no more tears or sorrow, pain or death . . . no heartaches, no handicaps, no grief, no sickness, not even a brief moment of anxiety. Count on it, my Christian friend, once we make it to our final destination, we'll have it made!

But what about *until* then? Look again at the lyrics of that old gospel song. Observe where we are standing and casting "a wishful eye." We are on *the banks* . . . and they are *stormy.* We may be "bound for the promised land," but realistically, we find ourselves living on the rocky, slippery banks of a treacherous river where disappointment and disaster are commonplace and strong winds of adversity blow like mad.

TWO REALISTIC REMINDERS

As enjoyable as it would be to focus our attention on the idyllic scenes of "Canaan's fair and happy land," we must face the harsh realities of where we find ourselves today. The real-world existence that engages our time and effort is neither ideal nor easy, hence the need for strong determination. And since that is true, it might be helpful to consider a couple of reminders to ready us for life on the pioneer trail of reality. Both of them are based on a few comments made by the apostle Paul in his second letter to the Corinthians, chapter 4.

First, *opposition is inevitable*. Look at the following words carefully.

We are afflicted in every way, but not crushed; perplexed, but not despairing;

*persecuted, but not forsaken; struck
down, but not destroyed; always carry-
ing about in the body the dying of Jesus,
that the life of Jesus also may be mani-
fested in our body.* (2 Cor. 4:8–10)

As you examine those words,
underscore just the verbs in verse 8:
"afflicted," "perplexed," "persecuted,"
"struck down." Count on it . . .
those words are an apt description of
life on the trail. Back in the nineteenth century, in the days of wagon
trains and rugged trails and battles
with the elements, the "opposition"
was things like harsh weather, broken
axles, swollen rivers, muddy bogs,
Indian attacks, lost children, and

untimely deaths. It has been reported that an average of seventeen people died for every wagon-train mile.[2]

The opposition we face today is different from that and usually much more complicated. There are relational struggles, marital disharmonies, difficulties connected with rearing children and teens, and financial strains. There are also occupational trials, hardship, sickness, calamities, crises, and conflicts, to name only a few. My point? Such things are *inevitable*. There is no escaping the downside of life on the human plane.

While involved in conference ministry in the summer of 1991, I spoke on this very subject. Even though we were enjoying a great week together, I felt that all of us needed the reminder that life back home would be altogether different from that week we were spending together. I reminded everyone that the mail was stacking up, the temperature was rising, and things at the office or shop may not be going along as well as we may wish. I even mentioned the possibility of *plumbing problems* along with several other practical types of difficulties. As we sat together, all that seemed remote —almost wrong to mention—in our delightful conference week . . . but one of the couples in attendance soon discovered the truth of my warning.

When they arrived home late one night, they noticed water coming out from under their garage door. Upon entering, they were shocked to see that the ceiling above the dining room had fallen down across their lovely table and water was dripping from above. The carpets were soggy across the downstairs area and one section of their wall was soaking wet. Hurrying upstairs, they found that their master bedroom toilet had been running, had gotten stopped up, and had been overflowing for almost an entire week. They suddenly remembered my comment

about plumbing problems and won-
dered if I had the gift of prophecy.
No . . . no gift like that, just an
understanding of life's inevitabilities.
Opposition and difficulties, pain,
disappointment, and heartaches are
par for the course. Expect them.
That way you won't be caught off
guard when (not *if*) they occur.

Second, *motivation is essential.*

*Therefore we do not lose heart,
but though our outer man is decaying,
yet our inner man is being renewed day
by day. For momentary, light affliction
is producing for us an eternal weight
of glory far beyond all comparison,
while we look not at the things which*

*are seen, but at the things which are
not seen; for the things which are seen
are temporal, but the things which are
not seen are eternal.* (vv. 16–18)

How insightful! Everything within
us cries out, "Just quit!" when we
encounter life's irritations, one after
another. But the wise apostle's
counsel, "Don't lose heart," an-
nounces a better alternative. What
is it he suggests? An attitude of fortitude . . . the motivation of determination. There is nothing more
vital en route to the "Promised Land"
than the presence of a positive attitude, that never-say-die mentality,
regardless. Because I can assure you,

you will be surrounded by negative, petty, and pessimistic folks who will not only cave in themselves, but will want you to follow suit . . . and you will be tempted to do so, especially when problems multiply. And there will be days when they will not only multiply, they will divide.

This reminds me of a true story . . . happened to a woman in Darlington, Maryland several years ago.

[Edith, a mother of eight,] was coming home from a neighbor's house one Saturday afternoon. As she came nearer she saw five of her youngest children huddled together in great concentration of interest and effort. As she came near,

*all the time trying to discover the center
of attraction, she was aghast to see
them playing with baby skunks. She
screamed at the top of her voice, "Children, run!"* Each one grabbed a
skunk and ran![3]

NEHEMIAH:
PIONEER OF DETERMINATION

Having set the stage for our need
for determination, it's time we meet
the man who could have sat for a
portrait of this important trait. His
name was Nehemiah. Few people
in biblical times faced life more
realistically or endured its difficulties
more positively. Not one to run from

trouble, the man cinched up his belt and waded right in, determined to complete the task God led him to accomplish.

And what task was that? Building a wall around the ancient city of Jerusalem. For years his beloved Zion lay unprotected, covered with debris and the scars of a Babylonian invasion. "Long enough!" he thought. He loved his homeland, which inspired his passion to return and restore its wall, which was nothing more than a ribbon of ruins. With vision and courage and faith as his motivation, Nehemiah requested permission from his superior, the Persian king, Artaxerxes, to return and rebuild that wall.

The task was enormous. The odds against him were huge and numerous, as we shall see. Furthermore, those who volunteered to take on that project with him were neither skilled as stone masons nor paid for their services. And to add insult to injury, there were those who lived near the ruins who did not want that wall to be reconstructed. When you mix all that into the equation, you quickly realize that the one who led the construction project must have had endless energy fueled by a daily supply of determination. Enter: Nehemiah.

We pick up the story in the

second chapter of the biblical book that bears his name.

And I arose in the night, I and a few men with me. I did not tell anyone what my God was putting into my mind to do for Jerusalem and there was no animal with me except the animal on which I was riding. So I went out at night by the Valley Gate in the direction of the Dragon's Well and on to the Refuse Gate, inspecting the walls of Jerusalem which were broken down and its gates which were consumed by fire. Then I passed on to the Fountain Gate and the King's Pool, but there was no place for my mount to pass. So I went up at night by the ravine and inspected the wall. Then I entered the Valley Gate again and returned. And the officials did not know where I had gone or what I had done; nor had I as yet told the Jews, the priests, the nobles, the officials, or the rest who did the work. (Neh. 2:12–16)

And in case you are wondering how he motivated the people to put their shoulder to the wheel, keep reading.

Then I said to them, "You see the bad situation we are in, that Jerusalem is desolate and its gates burned by fire. Come, let us rebuild the wall of Jerusalem that we may no longer be

a reproach." And I told them how the hand of my God had been favorable to me, and also about the king's words which he had spoken to me. Then they said, "Let us arise and build." So they put their hands to the good work.
(vv. 17–18)

As you would expect, early on there was opposition.

But when Sanballat the Horonite, and Tobiah the Ammonite official, and Geshem the Arab heard it, they mocked us and despised us and said, "What is this thing you are doing? Are you rebelling against the king?" So I answered them and said to them, "The God of

heaven will give us success; therefore
we His servants will arise and build,
but you have no portion, right, or
memorial in Jerusalem." (vv. 19–20)

THREE OPPRESSIVE OBSTACLES

Since we have already established
that opposition is inevitable, we're
not surprised to find it here in
ancient Jerusalem. Nehemiah and
his fellow workers faced no less than
three different types of obstacles, each
one extremely tough to deal with.

Verbal Criticism.

Go back and read the nineteenth

and twentieth verses of Nehemiah 2, where three enemies of the faith spoke out against the project. You will recall that they mocked the construction crew, they spoke sarcastically, and they called their motive into question.

Furthermore, a bit later they demonstrated a growing attitude of hostility as their criticism intensified.

Now it came about that when Sanballat heard that we were rebuilding the wall, he became furious and very angry and mocked the Jews. And he spoke in the presence of his brothers and the wealthy men of Samaria and said, "What are these feeble Jews doing? Are they going to restore it for themselves? Can they offer sacrifices? Can they finish in a day? Can they revive the stones from the dusty rubble even the burned ones?" Now Tobiah the Ammonite was near him and he said, "Even what they are building—if a fox should jump on it, he would break their stone wall down!"

Hear, O our God, how we are despised! Return their reproach on their own heads and give them up for plunder in a land of captivity. Do not forgive their iniquity and let not their sin be blotted out before Thee. (4:1–5a)

Those who criticize sometimes go for the jugular, as these men did.

As nay-sayers, they focus on what
won't happen, what *can't* get done,
and what *shouldn't* be attempted.
They jab. They shake their heads
and frown a lot. They emphasize
(and usually exaggerate) the difficulties connected with the project.
They harp on the negatives. And as
a result, they can demoralize those
who are in the arena of activity trying to get a big job done.

Nehemiah refused to let that
happen. Instead of allowing the critics to steal the zeal and/or silence
the joy of his workers, he stood firm
and kept his eyes on the goal. If
God had led him to rebuild that
wall, that is exactly what would get

accomplished, the opposition not-
withstanding. Return to his source
of strength momentarily.

So I answered them and said to them,
"The God of heaven will give us suc-
cess; therefore we His servants will
arise and build, but you have no por-
tion, right, or memorial in Jerusalem."
. . . So we built the wall and the whole
wall was joined together to half its
height, for the people had a mind to
work. (2:20; 4:6)

I love it! He took the criticism
to God in prayer . . . then returned
to the task at hand. In fact, they
found themselves halfway along

before they knew it! But did that stop the opposition? You know better than that. Like the skunks in Edith's home, the problems only intensified.

Now it came about when Sanballat, Tobiah, the Arabs, the Ammonites, and the Ashdodites heard that the repair of the walls of Jerusalem went on, and that the breaches began to be closed, they were very angry. And all of them conspired together to come and fight against Jerusalem and to cause a disturbance in it. (vv. 7–8)

A Secret Conspiracy.

The opposition went underground

and things started getting ugly.
Angry feelings spread like germs in
an infected area. A growing number
of people from the region joined
ranks with the critics. Notice that
their desire was "to cause a disturbance." Why, of course. Anything
to stop the project . . . and few
things are more effective than a
ground swell of hostility. Morale
can break down as a spirit of fear is
injected into the project. Feelings
of uneasiness can cut the heart out
of people's desire to stay at the task.

Knowing how quickly such feelings could invade and conquer,
Nehemiah prayed. But he did more
than that; he set up a counterstrat-

egy. We read of it here in the same chapter that told us of the secret conspiracy.

But we prayed to our God, and because of them we set up a guard against them day and night. Thus in Judah it was said,

> *"The strength of the burden*
> *bearers is failing,*
> *Yet there is much rubbish;*
> *And we ourselves are unable*
> *To rebuild the wall."*

And our enemies said, "They will not know or see until we come among them, kill them, and put a stop to the work." And it came about when the Jews who lived near them came and told us ten

times, "They will come up against us
from every place where you may turn,"
then I stationed men in the lowest parts
of the space behind the wall, the exposed
places, and I stationed the people in
families with their swords, spears, and
bows. When I saw their fear, I rose
and spoke to the nobles, the officials,
and the rest of the people: "Do not be
afraid of them; remember the Lord who
is great and awesome, and fight for
your brothers, your sons, your daugh-
ters, your wives, and your houses."

And it happened when our enemies
heard that it was known to us, and
that God had frustrated their plan, then
all of us returned to the wall, each one
to his work. And it came about from

*that day on, that half of my servants
carried on the work while half of them
held the spears, the shields, the bows,
and the breastplates; and the captains
were behind the whole house of Judah.
Those who were rebuilding the wall
and those who carried burdens took
their load with one hand doing the work
and the other holding a weapon. As
for the builders, each wore his sword
girded at his side as he built, while the
trumpeter stood near me. And I said
to the nobles, the officials, and the rest
of the people, "The work is great and
extensive, and we are separated on the
wall far from one another. At whatever
place you hear the sound of the trum-
pet, rally to us there. Our God will*

fight for us."

*So we carried on the work with
half of them holding spears from dawn
until the stars appeared. At that time I
also said to the people, "Let each man
with his servant spend the night within
Jerusalem so that they may be a guard
for us by night and a laborer by day."
So neither I, my brothers, my servants,
nor the men of the guard who followed
me, none of us removed our clothes,
each took his weapon even to the water.*
(vv. 9–23)

Smart! He didn't simply suggest,
"Let's trust the Lord." No, he set
up a plan—a balanced plan of
defense—to keep the enemy at bay

without hindering the progress of the project. *It worked!* This old pioneer of determination pulled them through that tough period by reminding the people that their *God* was great and awesome, not those who led the conspiracy.

How easy it is to forget our greatest source of protection and strength when we are being attacked. How common it is to fight back by our own efforts, based on our own human wisdom. Let me say this straight: Refuse to do that! Instead, pray, pray, pray, PRAY. As Jim Elliot, the martyred missionary, once wrote in his journal, "The saint who advances on his knees, never retreats."

Reminds me of our friend, Nehemiah: "O God, remember us." A little later, "O God, protect us." Then, "O God, strengthen us." After that, "O God, silence the enemy." Woven through the fabric of this book, which is in effect Nehemiah's journal, is a veritable network of intercession and petition. And as the man advances on his knees, the wall continues going up. As God is given the green light to fight our battles, it is amazing how He brings fresh determination. But is that a guarantee that all opposition will end? Not on your life.

A Clever Deception.

What happened next was the most insidious attack on the project thus far. An "open letter" was used to intimidate, after Nehemiah refused to cooperate with the enemy's nice-sounding request. We read of all this in the sixth chapter of the book.

Now it came about when it was reported to Sanballat, Tobiah, to Geshem the Arab, and to the rest of our enemies that I had rebuilt the wall, and that no breach remained in it, although at that time I had not set up the doors in the gates, that Sanballat and Geshem sent a message to me, saying, "Come, let us meet together at Chephirim in the plain of Ono." But they were planning to harm me. So I sent messengers to them, saying, "I am doing a great work and I cannot come down. Why should the work stop while I leave it and come down to you?" And they sent messages to me four times in this manner, and I answered them in the same way. Then Sanballat sent his servant to me in the same manner a fifth time with an open letter in his hand. In it was written, "It is reported among the nations, and Gashmu says, that you and the Jews are planning to rebel; therefore you are rebuilding the wall. And you are to be their king, according to these *reports. And you have also appointed prophets to proclaim in Jerusalem concerning you, 'A king is in Judah!' And now it will be reported to the king according to these reports. So come now, let us take counsel together."* (6:1–7)

How wise of Nehemiah not to play into the hands of his conspirators! Yet his refusal infuriated the opposition party, which prompted them to write an infamous "open letter" full of lies and rumor. By questioning his motive ("you . . . are planning to rebel . . . you are to be their king") they hoped to instill fear in Nehemiah and distrust among his workers. Planning secretly to do him harm, they invited him to meet with them on neutral turf. They dropped the lure and gave it a subtle shake.

Nehemiah didn't bite. Instead, he exposed *their* motive and announced *their* hidden agenda.

Then I sent a message to him saying, "Such things as you are saying have not been done, but you are inventing them in your own mind." For all of them were trying to frighten us, thinking, "They will become discouraged with the work and it will not be done." But now, O God, strengthen my hands. . . . But I said, "Should a man like me flee? And could one such as I

*go into the temple to save his life? I
will not go in." Then I perceived that
surely God had not sent him, but he
uttered his prophecy against me because
Tobiah and Sanballat had hired him.
He was hired for this reason, that I
might become frightened and act accord-
ingly and sin, so that they might have
an evil report in order that they could
reproach me. Remember, O my God,
Tobiah and Sanballat according to these
works of theirs, and also Noadiah the
prophetess and the rest of the prophets
who were trying to frighten me.*
(vv. 8–9, 11–14)

I often think of those immortal
words of Winston Churchill when I

hear or read of someone's standing victoriously against others' attacks.

Nothing in life is so exhilarating as to be shot at without result.[4]

This pioneer of determination saw through their schemes and stood his ground. And the best news of all?

So the wall was completed on the twenty-fifth of the month Elul, in fifty-two days. (v. 15)

Look at that and smile big! He finished the task. What Nehemiah's God had led him to do, He enabled him to complete. From start to finish, God was in control. God initiated the idea and placed it on Nehemiah's heart. God built a fire beneath the idea and Nehemiah's passion grew to the boiling point. God opened the mind of the king in Persia, who released Nehemiah to travel to Jerusalem and superintend the construction project. God gave the people under Nehemiah's leadership a strong desire to work. God protected them from physical attack and the breakdown of morale. God heard Nehemiah's many prayers and granted his requests. Finally, God gave both leader and workmen the wisdom and the skill and the stamina to see the project through

to completion. In the meantime,
the enemy was silenced, and guess
who got the glory. Why of course,
God! Had they had the hymn in
those ancient days, they would surely
have sung, "To God be the glory—
great things He hath done!"[5]

A FEW CLOSING WORDS
OF MOTIVATION

Stretching out before us are vast
frontiers yet to be conquered. Time
nor space allow me an opportunity
to list them. But you know which
ones represent your *personal* "frontiers." To deal with them as you
must, a pioneer spirit is not merely

an option—it's essential. Frontiers
require pioneers . . . people who
will not quit, who refuse to take
the easy road of escape or compromise. Frontiers represent rugged
places, lonely journeys, fierce battles, harsh and heavy demands. As I
said at the beginning, thin-skinned
soldiers need not apply. You will be
tested to the extremity of your te-
nacity . . . but God will honor in
you what He honored in Nehemiah:
determination.

Here are four helpful hints for
frontier living. I want you to do more
than read them and think about
them. I suggest you *memorize* them
and *personalize* them. Write them

on a three-by-five card or a post-it
and stick them on the mirror in your
bathroom so you can review them
every morning until they become a
part of your everyday mind-set.

1. Never let life's difficulties surprise
   you.
   We have learned that hardship,
disappointments, and struggles are
inevitable. They *will* happen. They
are the rule, not the exceptions, of
life. So? So, begin your day by moni-
toring your expectations. Force yourself to be realistic instead of idealis-
tic. Anticipate the challenge ahead
of you as you enter new frontiers
each day will bring, and . . .

2. Keep a positive perspective.

Rather than dreading each dawn, rehearse your objectives in the morning and remind yourself that God is awesome . . . in full control. As the day unfolds, focus on your goal just as Nehemiah focused on the building of that wall. Nothing dissuaded him from that all-important pursuit . . . no criticism, no conspiracy, no clever scheme, nothing. And instead of allowing the negativism he faced to occupy his mind, he kept a positive perspective. In order for that to happen . . .

3. Fight your fiercest battles on your knees.

We have found that Nehemiah's journal is punctuated with prayers. He prayed for help. You must do the same. He prayed for protection. So must you. He prayed for wisdom . . . for strength . . . for God's interventions. Like Nehemiah, keep your prayers short, specific, and spontaneous. Don't wait until Sunday rolls around to get "caught up" . . . mix brief moments of prayer into your everyday encounters. Don't try to handle the blows of life all alone. You need help outside yourself, which means you need to . . .

4. Stay close to others.
God never meant for us to be

lone rangers. None of us is totally
self-sufficient. When you study the
lives and lifestyles of settlers and
pioneers of yesteryear, you discover
that they quickly learned the value
of staying close. Shortly after acquir-
ing land, they built their sod huts
in the middle of their acreage, but
they found that that left them vul-
nerable and exposed. When they
needed help it was too far away,
which usually spelled disaster. They
learned to build their homes at the
corner of their property, not too far
from their neighbors, who built on
the corner of theirs as well. A
"cluster" of homes built in fairly close
proximity made a lot more sense

when threats arose from enemy attack
or sickness invaded or fire broke
out. Furthermore, life became more
enjoyable when its blessings and its
hardships were not experienced
alone. As the old Swedish proverb
states it, "Shared joy is a double joy;
shared sorrow is half a sorrow."[6]

May these words bring you reas-
surance and renew your determination as you continue living your days
"on Jordan's stormy banks." And
may these final four principles keep
you strong when the storm is especially violent and the tests seem
especially severe.

Dear Lord,

The realization that we are pioneers is both exciting and excruciating. A part of us responds with a smile, another part recoils in fear. Something deep within welcomes the challenge, knowing that it is through hard times we grow toward maturity. As the hymnwriter put it, we are not "carried to the skies on flow'ry beds of ease."[7] *The journey to Canaan's land is a rugged one, full of tests that could harm us and trials that can hurt us.*

Give us the determination of Nehemiah. Enable us to stay strong, focused, firm. Cultivate within us a quiet confidence in Your sovereign control regardless of the Sanballats and Tobiahs and Geshems who cross our paths. Guard us from bitterness. And most of all, take the word "quit" from our vocabulary.

We don't know what frontiers we'll be facing, but we know You. And so, we rest in You as our Shield and our Defender. Be that and more, faithful Father, for we need You desperately, as we are bound for the Promised Land.

In the powerful name of Your Son, Jesus, Amen.

NOTES

1. Samuel Stennett, "On Jordan's Stormy Banks," in *The Hymnal for Worship and Celebration* (Waco, Tex.: Word Music, 1986), no. 552.

2. Louis L'Amour, *Frontier* (New York, N.Y.: Bantam Books, 1984), p. 84.

3. John Edmund Haggai, *How to Win Over Worry* (Grand Rapids, Mich.: Zondervan Publishing House, 1959), p. 144.

4. *Bartlett's Familiar Quotations*, 15th ed., rev. and enl., ed. Emily Morison Beck (Boston, Mass.: Little, Brown and Co., 1980), p. 743.

5. Fanny J. Crosby, "To God Be the Glory," in *The Hymnal for Worship and Celebration*, no. 66.

6. Bruce Larson, *There's a Lot More to Health Than Not Being Sick* (Waco, Tex.: Word Books, 1981), p. 60.

7. Isaac Watts, "Am I A Soldier of the Cross?," in *The Hymnal for Worship and Celebration*, no. 482.